Aaron's Day Off

By Cindy M.

Illustrated by Rupert Van Wyk

Copyright© Cindy Mackey, 2017

Illustrations copyright© Rupert Van Wyk, 2017

Graphic Design by: Hannah Mackey, 2017

All rights reserved. This book or any
portion thereof may not be reproduced
or used in any manner whatsoever
without the express written permission
of the publisher.

Published in the United States of America by:
Cyrano Books
918 12th Avenue, Suite 1000
Honolulu, HI 96816

www.cyranobooks.com

For Aaron

This is Aaron.

Aaron is an immensely capable boy.

He can milk three cows at once,

pluck ten chickens in under a minute,

chase down a runaway calf,

drive a tractor like an expert,

and build a house in a single day.

Aaron is good at so many things that no one has ever counted all the things he can do!

In fact, Aaron is so capable that everyone in town wants him to work for them.

Every day after school and on weekends,
Aaron spends his time ...

milking cows, plucking chickens, chasing down a calf, driving a tractor, building a house, and more things than anyone can count!

But one day, the whole town decided to take a day off.

Aaron didn't want to take a day off, so he got on his bike and went in search of something to do.

It didn't take long for Aaron to find people who could use his help.

So he helped...

and helped...

and helped...

and helped.

By the end of the day, Aaron was ready to go home.

Before he left, a little boy asked Aaron,
"Are you a superhero? Like *The Flash* or *Superman*?"

Aaron shook his head, "No."

"Then how can you do so many things, so well?"

Aaron smiled and said,
"Because no one told me I couldn't."

The End.

www.ingramcontent.com/pod-product-compliance
Lightning Source LLC
Chambersburg PA
CBHW041125300426
44113CB00002B/59